Deadliest Sharks

Melissa Abramovitz

San Diego, CA

ReferencePoint
Press®

© 2017 ReferencePoint Press, Inc.
Printed in the United States

For more information, contact:
ReferencePoint Press, Inc.
PO Box 27779
San Diego, CA 92198
www.ReferencePointPress.com

LIBRARY OF CONGRESS CATALOGING-IN-PUBLICATION DATA

Names: Abramovitz, Melissa, 1954- . author.
Title: Deadliest sharks / by Melissa Abramovitz.
Description: San Diego, CA : ReferencePoint Press, Inc., 2017. | Series:
    Deadliest predators | Includes bibliographical references and index. |
    Audience: Grades 7-8.
Identifiers: LCCN 2015050838 (print) | LCCN 2016021116 (ebook) | ISBN
    9781682820544 (hardback) | ISBN 9781682820551 (epub)
Subjects: LCSH: Sharks--Juvenile literature.
Classification: LCC QL638.9 .A27 2017 (print) | LCC QL638.9 (ebook) | DDC
    597.3--dc23
LC record available at https://lccn.loc.gov/2015050838

Contents

Apex Predators

Sharks are among the most feared animals on Earth. When they attack humans, the results can be horrific. However, biologists point out that many of the approximately four hundred known species of sharks are not dangerous to people. Attacks by sharks that are dangerous to humans are rare as well. The International Shark Attack File (ISAF) reports that there have been 2,778 confirmed unprovoked shark attacks worldwide between 1580 and 2014. Of these attacks, 497 were fatal. Unprovoked means that people did nothing to frighten or otherwise bother the shark. There have been thousands more provoked attacks, and many others that were unconfirmed or unreported. Even so, the chances of being attacked or killed by a shark are about one in 3 million. In comparison, the chances of drowning at sea are about a thousand times higher.

When sharks do attack humans, it is because these people are in the shark's territory. Sharks do not set out to kill or eat humans. They are simply ideally designed meat-eating predators doing what they do best—hunting and eating. Indeed, sharks have been around for at least 350 million years because they have qualities that let them reign supreme in their habitat.

Biologists call sharks apex predators—those that are at the top of the food chain. According to the National

Oceanic and Atmospheric Administration, apex predators eat "many species lower on the food chain, have few natural predators themselves, and are less abundant than their prey."[1] Sharks have evolved various methods of achieving the status of apex predators.

What Makes Sharks Apex Predators?

Many people wrongly believe that sharks are apex predators because they are vicious, mindless eating machines. Their huge teeth and the ability of these teeth to grow back when one is lost or damaged help make them ferocious predators. But the sharks' body design, along with their large brains, is equally responsible for their success as hunters. The shark skeleton, which is made of lightweight, flexible cartilage, helps sharks move quickly. This allows many types of sharks to outswim and catch their prey. Sharks' brains also play a big role in finding and attacking the animals on which they feed.

Sharks' brains are comparable in size to those of birds and mammals, which biologists consider to be the most intelligent animals. Areas of the shark brain that receive and analyze information from the sense organs are especially well developed. Cells in the sense organs that detect smells, sounds, sights, and two special senses that humans lack are especially important in alerting sharks' brains to the presence and direction of prey animals.

One special sensory system is the lateral line. It consists of tubes on both sides of the body that contain pressure-sensitive cells. When something in the water moves, this changes the water pressure, causing water to flow into the tubes through pores in the shark's skin. These cells are similar to pressure-sensitive cells in the shark's ears. Together, the cells in the lateral line and

A bull shark (top, center) swims with other fish and sharks in a lagoon in Fiji, an archipelago in the South Pacific. Sharks are at the top of the food chain in their ocean habitats.

ears feed information to the brain that lets sharks detect sounds and other water pressure changes miles away.

The second special sense is called electroreception. This sense lets sharks detect tiny electric signals given off by the muscles of all living creatures. Electroreception depends on clusters of cells called the ampullae of Lorenzini. These clusters are named after the man who discovered them—the seventeenth-century Italian physician and fish biologist Stefano Lorenzini.

The ampullae are located under the skin in the shark's head. Each ampulle is filled with a gel that conducts electricity and signals the brain that electric fields are present in a specific location.

Dangers to Sharks and Oceans

The tools that make sharks apex predators contribute to the critical role they play in keeping the balance of nature in the oceans where they live. However, this balance is seriously threatened because people have overfished and otherwise killed sharks for many years. This has reduced the number of sharks so much that populations of animals they ordinarily eat, such as seals, have increased significantly. More seals eat more fish, leaving fewer fish for other sea life. The same thing happens with other species sharks eat, and the effects reverberate down the food chain.

Shark populations have decreased so much that biologists consider at least one-fourth of the known shark species to be endangered (having a very high risk of extinction), vulnerable (having a high risk of extinction), or near threatened (close to qualifying as endangered or vulnerable). In response to these shark population decreases, many countries throughout the world have enacted laws that prohibit killing sharks. However, many people ignore these laws and continue to kill many types of sharks out of fear or for their meat, fins (for sharkfin soup), skin (for leatherlike products), teeth (for souvenirs), and livers (for oil used in cosmetics, medicines, and other products). Experts estimate that people kill 2 million sharks for every human killed by a shark.

As shark experts Leonard Compagno and Sarah Fowler explain in *Sharks of the World*, with all the hype about sharks being a danger to humans, "the true story of man and sharks is not one of man-eating sharks, but of the hugely more common shark-eating man. Sharks, not mankind, are the species in danger, the animals now being driven rapidly towards extinction."[2]

Conservation scientists and educators have launched programs to educate people about the need to protect sharks and to enact stricter conservation laws. These programs are starting to have an effect in that some shark populations are gradually increasing. However, rebuilding these numbers takes a long time because sharks reproduce slowly. Many species, like the great white shark, cannot reproduce until around age twenty, and they only produce two to ten offspring every few years. Thus, biologists expect shark populations and the balance of nature in the oceans to remain threatened for many years.

Chapter 1

Great White Shark

The great white shark is one of the most feared animals in the world. It is responsible for more shark-related attacks and deaths in humans than any other type of shark—more than four hundred attacks and at least seventy deaths. The name *great white* comes from the shark's huge size and white belly.

Great White Basics

The great white has a heavy, muscular, torpedo-shaped body with black eyes, a pointed snout, two dorsal (upper) fins, a crescent-shaped tail, and large gill openings. Its mouth contains twenty to thirty triangular, serrated teeth about 3 inches (7.6 cm) long in each of several rows in the upper jaw and the same number of longer, pointed teeth in the lower jaw. The body coloring is gray to brownish, bluish, or bronze on top and white underneath. These sharks are usually 13 to 20 feet (4 to 6 m) long and weigh 2,200 to 4,400 pounds (998 to 1,996 kg), though there are reports of great whites as long as 26 feet (8 m).

At Home in the Sea

The great white lives in cool to warm ocean waters worldwide, from shallow coastal waters to open ocean areas. It prefers water temperatures between 54°F and 75°F (12°C to 24°C) and usually stays near the surface down to about 4,000 feet (1,220 m). The great white is comfortable in cool as well as warm water because unlike most fish, it is warm-blooded.

The greatest concentrations of great whites are in the Atlantic and Pacific Oceans near the United States and in the Atlantic, Pacific, and Indian Oceans near South Africa, Japan, Chile, Oceania, and Australia. They are also prevalent in the Mediterranean Sea. These sharks are often seen near seal and walrus colonies in all these places. They migrate great distances to find these and other favorite prey. In fact, scientists who attached a satellite tracking device to the upper fin of a great white they named Katherine found that she traveled more than 14,000 miles (22,530 km) between August 2013 and July 2015.

Finding Prey

The great white preys on a variety of large fish like tuna and smaller sharks and on octopus, squid, rays, sea birds, sea turtles, and marine mammals like seals and dolphins. It usually hunts at dawn and dusk but also sometimes during the day, using its well-developed senses of smell, hearing, vision, lateral line, and electro-reception to find food. Most areas of the great white's large brain are devoted to processing information sent by its sensory organs and to directing the shark to track down prey. A 15-foot (4.6 m) great white's brain is about 2 feet (60 cm) long. As biologist Steve Parker explains in *The Encyclopedia of Sharks*, a brain this large "is often said to reflect what we term 'intelligence.'"[3] However, the shark's intelligence centers on being an apex predator, not on humanlike activities like computer design.

When hunting for food, the great white shark (pictured) depends on its muscular, torpedo-shaped body for speed and power. With its keen sense of smell, the shark can locate prey through the scent of an animal's blood or urine.

At a distance, the senses of hearing, lateral line, and smell are important in helping the shark sense prey. Its lateral line and ears are sensitive to changes in water pressure created by animals moving miles away. These systems are especially sensitive to distress sounds,

THE GREAT WHITE SHARK AT A GLANCE

- **Scientific name:** *Carcharodon carcharias*
- **Scientific family:** Lamnidae
- **Range:** Worldwide
- **Habitat:** Warm to cool waters; coastal areas to open ocean
- **Size:** Usually 13 to 20 feet (4 to 6 m)
- **Weight:** Usually 2,200 to 4,400 pounds (998 to 1,996 kg)
- **Key features:** Torpedo-shaped body; pointed snout; gray to brownish, bluish, or bronze color on top; white underneath
- **Diet:** Large fish like tuna and smaller sharks; rays, octopus, squid, marine mammals, sea birds, sea turtles
- **Deadly because:** Teeth, speed, camouflage, aggression, huge appetite
- **Life span:** As long as 70 years
- **Conservation status:** Vulnerable

such as thrashing around, that signify a sick or injured animal. The shark responds aggressively to such signals because this means an easy catch with less chance of self-injury or of an exhausting pursuit.

The shark also responds aggressively to smells such as blood that signal a wounded animal. While humans can smell a variety of substances, the sensory cells in great whites' (and most other sharks) nostrils only respond to substances like blood and urine that are associated with animals' body functions. Great whites' nasal cells are especially sensitive to blood. They can smell one drop of blood floating in ten billion drops of water from 3 miles (5 km) away. The shark's brain also compares the strength of the smells in each nostril to determine the animal's location. With these sensitive tools, "If you're alive, the great white can find you,"[4] states *The Big Book of Sharks*.

Going After Prey

Once a great white senses a possible meal, it quickly swims to find the animal. It can swim as fast as 35 miles per hour (56 kph)—the speed reached by a car on a city street. Several factors contribute to the shark's speed. Fast swimming requires a great deal of energy, which the shark obtains from food and oxygen. The lungs take in oxygen from the water through the gills and mouth, and the shark's large heart pumps this oxygen throughout the body via the bloodstream. Much of this oxygen feeds the huge muscles that push the shark ahead and the digestive system that processes food and sends nutrients throughout the body.

Besides relying on energy from food and oxygen, the shark achieves fast speeds due to its warm-bloodedness. Being warm-blooded keeps the muscles warm; warm muscles move faster and more easily than cold ones. Having a flexible cartilage skeleton also helps the shark move quickly because it lets the body bend while swimming and allows the shark to turn quickly in tight circles. This allows it to literally run circles around and catch its prey.

Other factors contribute to the great white's speed by reducing drag from the water. Drag is resistance cre-

The razor-sharp, serrated tooth of a great white shark cuts into flesh like a saw. When a tooth breaks or falls out, another tooth moves forward to take its place.

ated by the surrounding environment that slows down a moving object. One category of factors that reduce drag is the great white's teardrop-shaped body, crescent-shaped tail, and long, narrow pectoral (chest) fins. Narrow, tapered objects occupy less space than wider ones, and this reduces drag by decreasing the area the water pushes against. The pectoral fins and tail also work like oars that push water aside while pushing the shark ahead. In addition, toothlike scales called dermal denticles on the shark's skin also reduce drag by pushing water aside. The denticles make the skin very tough, which protects the shark from injury during struggles with prey. Even without a struggle, the great white needs tough skin because when it barrels at full speed into its prey, biologists describe the impact as comparable to being hit by a speeding train.

Besides speed, great whites' so-called spy-hopping behavior also helps them hunt, particularly when the prey is on the water's surface. In spy hopping, the shark holds itself vertical with its head out of the water to look for prey. Unlike some sharks, the great white has good vision, and having one eye on each side of the head allows it to see all around itself.

The Attack

Vision also plays a role in the great white's final approach to underwater prey. Its eyes usually guide it to a place underneath the animal, and it shoots upward to grab it. The attack usually surprises the prey because the shark's body coloring provides camouflage. The dark color on top and the white underside break up the body outline when seen from above or below because of the way the sun hits the water.

In April 2015 scientists at Flinders University in Australia published a study that shows how great whites instinctively enhance this natural camouflage. The researchers found that great whites attack from different directions at different hours of the day, depending on the angle of the sun. The shark approaches its prey so the sun is directly behind itself. At dawn, it usually approaches from the east. At dusk, it approaches from the west. On cloudy days, these preferences disappear. The Flinders biologists believe these studies explain why great whites usually hunt at dusk and dawn, when the sun's angle is lowest in the sky. The sun therefore casts very little light on the shark.

As the shark races to snare its prey, its speed often causes it to breach, or jump out of, the water. It then splashes down and grabs the animal with its huge lower teeth. When it bites into the animal, its eyes automatically roll back in their sockets for protection in case of a struggle. Unable to see at this point, the shark depends on electroreception to track the prey if it struggles or tries to escape. The approximately fifteen hundred ampullae of Lorenzini in the snout and mouth areas let the great white accurately pinpoint the prey up to about 3 feet (90 cm) away.

After biting the animal, the shark saws off flesh with its sawlike upper teeth while flinging its head from side to side. This can be hard on the teeth, but if a tooth breaks or falls out, another that sits in the rows of teeth eventually moves forward to take its place.

Is It a Man-Eater?

Great whites' proficiency as predators has led to many misconceptions about them. One reason for these misconceptions is that biologists used to call them killing machines. Then, the 1974 book and 1975 movie *Jaws*, which featured a ferocious great white, enhanced peoples' terror. *Jaws* was based on a series of shark attacks that killed four people at the New Jersey shore in 1916. After these attacks, many seaside communities built steel nets around public beaches to protect

A WARM-BLOODED SHARK

Being warm-blooded increases the great white's efficiency as an apex predator. Most sharks are cold-blooded. That is, their body temperature matches the temperature of the surrounding water. The body temperature of great whites stays 10°F to 20°F (-12°C to -7°C) warmer than the water temperature because of three sets of mesh-like networks of blood vessels called retia mirabilia. These networks warm the blood coming from the heart before it gets to the swimming muscles, the internal body organs, and the eyes and brain. This increases the speed and strength of the muscles, the speed of digestion and distribution of energy from food, and the alertness of the brain. It also allows great whites to inhabit colder water and to thus survive in a variety of environments.

Studies show that when the blood is 18°F (-8°C) warmer than the outside water, the swimming muscles can work three times harder and faster than normal. Thus, the shark can swim much faster than its cold-blooded prey. However, generating this warmth uses extra energy, so the shark must take in more food to convert to energy. This helps explain great whites' voracious appetites.

swimmers. The US Coast Guard even offered rewards to people who killed sharks.

Since then, biologists have learned that great whites do not set out to eat people. Some scientists believe great whites go after humans because they mistake

In pursuit of prey, a great white shark breaches or jumps out of the water. Once it has captured the animal, the shark's eyes roll back in their sockets for protection in case of a struggle.

people for seals or sea turtles, especially when the shark is underneath an individual on a surfboard. However, this theory has not been proved. What is known is that great whites find humans unappetizing because people do not have enough flesh for their taste. Many times a great white will take a test bite and leave after realizing the person is unappetizing. However, these bites can still do major damage because of the sharks' huge, razor-sharp teeth.

Most of the time, people get bitten or killed because they do things that attract great whites. Swimming with an open sore or urinating in the water often provokes an aggressive attack. So does splashing around, because it signals that an animal is hurt or sick. Swimming with dolphins puts people in danger because great whites like to eat these creatures. Sharks are also likely to attack spearfishing divers because these weapons make them feel threatened. And when people wear brightly colored clothing underwater, this attracts sharks because they are naturally drawn to contrasting colors. Experts recommend that humans educate themselves about shark behavior to protect themselves when they venture into shark habitats.

Chapter 2

Tiger Shark

The tiger shark is very aggressive and attacks more people than any other shark except the great white. The ISAF reports that there have been at least eighty unprovoked nonfatal tiger shark attacks and at least forty fatal attacks on humans between 1580 and 2014. However, experts suspect this number is actually higher because it is often impossible to confirm the species of an attacking shark. Many victims are unfamiliar with the tiger shark, and biologists believe some tiger shark attacks are misidentified as great white attacks. One fact that has been confirmed is that tiger sharks are responsible for most of the shark attacks in Australia and Hawaii.

One characteristic that makes the tiger shark especially dangerous is that it will eat anything (and is known as the garbage can of the sea). Bottles, tires, clothing, license plates, hubcaps, women's handbags, sacks of coal, and whole cats and pigs (sometimes snatched off boats or shallow-water docks) are just some of the items and animals that have been found in tiger shark stomachs. *The Encyclopedia of Sharks* explains that the willingness to eat anything makes tiger sharks "extremely successful large predators"[5] that can survive in ocean environments which contain a variety of creatures.

Tiger Shark Basics

The tiger shark is gray-green to gray-blue to black on top, with a pale underside that can be cream colored, light gray, white, or yellowish. It gets its name from the vertical stripes on young tiger sharks' skin. These stripes, along with the spots that many young tiger sharks also have, fade as the shark ages.

This shark has a large head with a blunt, rounded snout, five gill openings, and several rows of large, curved, serrated teeth in the lower and upper jaws. The body has two dorsal fins and exceptionally thick, tough skin. In fact, biologists state that its skin is six to ten times thicker than an ox hide, which is known to be extremely tough.

Tiger sharks usually range from 12 to 18 feet (3.7 to 5.5 m) long and weigh up to 1,400 pounds (635 kg). However, individuals as long as 25 feet (7.6 m), weighing as much as 3,000 pounds (1361 kg), have been found.

At Home in the Sea

The tiger shark lives in tropical and subtropical ocean waters worldwide, from coastal areas to open ocean areas. Given its liking for warm water, it is usually found in the southern hemisphere, though tiger sharks are also seen in waters off the southern parts of the United States and Central America. It stays in open ocean areas down to about 1,000 feet (305 m) during the day and moves to shallow coastal waters at night. The shark is often found in harbors and estuaries (shallow water areas between oceans and rivers that have a low salt content) as well.

Hunting Habits

The tiger shark eats anything and everything. Besides eating inedible objects, it also consumes dead animals, poisonous sea snakes, sea birds, sea mammals, turtles, eels, octopus, squid, stingrays, shellfish, and other sharks. Before birth, aggressive tiger shark fetuses often eat their sibling fetuses in the mother's womb. After birth, they eat their surviving newborn siblings as well. Scien-

Vertical stripes, visible on the upper body, mark the tiger shark. Experts say tiger sharks are responsible for most of the shark attacks in Australia and Hawaii.

THE TIGER SHARK
AT A GLANCE

- **Scientific name:** *Galeocerdo cuvier*
- **Scientific family:** Carcharhinidae
- **Range:** Worldwide
- **Habitat:** Tropical and subtropical ocean waters; coastal areas to open ocean
- **Size:** Usually 12 to 18 feet (3.7 to 5.5 m)
- **Weight:** Usually up to 1,400 pounds (635 kg)
- **Key features:** Large, curved, serrated teeth; gray-green to gray-blue to black color on top, paler color underneath; spots or stripes on young sharks' skin fade with age
- **Diet:** Dead animals, poisonous sea snakes, sea birds, sea mammals, turtles, eels, octopus, squid, other sharks, shellfish
- **Deadly because:** Teeth, aggression, eats anything
- **Life span:** Up to about 50 years
- **Conservation status:** Near threatened

tists do not know why the tiger shark is not affected by the potent poisons found in sea snakes, stingrays, and eels. In fact, highly poisonous sea snakes seem to be one of tiger sharks' favorite foods.

This shark usually hunts alone at night, using its strong senses of smell, hearing, sight, lateral line, and electroreception to find prey. However, when plenty of food is available, large groups of tiger sharks have been seen hunting together. Tiger sharks also may alter their usual habit of hunting and feeding at night when it gives them access to more food. For example, tiger sharks in Hawaii like to eat monk seals, which mostly hang out in the water during the day. So tiger sharks in this area hunt and feed during the day.

The tiger shark's huge appetite also motivates it to swim 30 to 40 miles (48 to 64 km) per day looking for food. As with the great white, the scent of blood or other body fluids is most likely to lure the tiger shark to a possible meal. Unlike the great white, however, the tiger shark does not swim quickly to reach far-away prey. It swims slowly until it spots the prey. Biologists believe tiger sharks cannot swim as fast as some sharks over long distances because the tiger shark's upper tail fin is much larger than the lower tail fin. This prevents the tail from pushing the shark ahead as efficiently as tails in which the upper and lower lobes are identical.

The tiger shark is, however, capable of swimming quickly in short bursts. After spotting a prey animal, the shark often inspects it from a distance and circles around it slowly before suddenly charging and attacking it. These bursts of speed can exceed 20 miles per hour (32 kph).

The Attack

The tiger shark often grabs and gulps down its prey in one bite. If it cannot swallow a whole animal in one bite, it often uses its wide snout to either stun or push the prey into a place (such as between two large rocks) that holds it while the shark tears off chunks to eat. Sometimes it simply holds the creature with its teeth while it saws off swallowable chunks.

A sea turtle carcass provides an easy meal for a tiger shark in the waters off Australia. Turtles, birds, eels, and even venomous sea snakes are tiger shark favorites.

The shark's large, curved, serrated teeth are ideally suited to saw through prey or objects it wishes to eat. The teeth let it slice through the shells of animals like sea turtles and crabs and through the tough skin of other sharks and sea mammals. In fact, tiger shark teeth are so sharp and tough that they easily crack hard shells

THE DEADLIEST SHARK ATTACK IN HISTORY

The tiger shark and another aggressive species, the oceanic whitetip, were responsible for what historians call the deadliest shark attack on humans in history. When the USS *Indianapolis* was hit by an enemy torpedo and sank in the Pacific Ocean in 1945, hundreds of sailors were attacked by sharks. Drawn by the smell of blood and noise from the blast, the sharks ate the bodies of men who died in the explosion. As more and more sharks arrived, they began attacking the living, who were staying afloat with life jackets. Four days later, a navy plane spotted the approximately three hundred survivors, and a seaplane and a ship were dispatched to rescue them.

This incident highlights what happens during a shark feeding frenzy. Biologists find that shark behavior can be influenced more by the actions of other sharks than by hunger. After a meal many sharks cruise around slowly and only go after easy prey. But if other sharks are detected feeding nearby, a shark often becomes more aggressive and starts eating everything in sight. Scientists think this behavior may result from the fear of competition for available food.

like conches. The unique shape of the teeth, which are identical in the upper and lower jaws, helps with this process. One side of each tooth has a large curve and is extremely sharp, sort of like a can opener blade. It is also serrated like a saw blade. The other side of each tooth has a smaller serrated curve. The shark first bites into its prey with the larger side of its teeth to break into shells or tough skin. Then it saws off chunks of flesh from larger animals using the smaller side of the teeth.

Tiger shark mouths are also proportionately wider than those of other sharks, and this helps them consume fairly large creatures all at once. In fact, a tiger shark caught in Australia had an intact, unchewed, horse head in its stomach (probably grabbed while it was wading or drinking in shallow water).

If any type of prey tries to escape, the tiger shark will aggressively pursue it until it catches up and can attack again. Its aggressive nature also leads it to fearlessly attack creatures that are bigger than itself. Few predators would dare to challenge the tiger shark. The primary exception is the killer whale.

Dangers to Humans

The tiger shark's aggressiveness and willingness to eat anything and everything also makes it dangerous to people. When tiger sharks attack humans, the individual is likely to die because the shark does not taste and spit out prey it finds unpalatable like the great white does. Indeed, some experts believe the tiger shark is more dangerous than the great white for this reason.

Sometimes people who have been attacked by these sharks do survive. One such person is surfer Bethany Hamilton. In 2003 at the age of thirteen, Hamilton was relaxing on her surfboard in Kauai, Hawaii, when a 15-foot (4.6 m) tiger shark bit off her arm. Friends quickly helped her to shore and applied a tourniquet to her shoulder. She still lost over 60 percent of her blood before arriving

The uniquely curved teeth of the tiger shark (pictured) enable the shark to cut into tough skin and shells much like a can opener blade. The sharp, serrated edges of the teeth allow the shark to saw through flesh.

at a hospital. Hamilton survived and began surfing again three weeks later. She went on to win several championships and awards, and inspired many people with her willingness to pursue her dreams after losing her arm.

Another characteristic that makes tiger sharks so dangerous to people is that they move to areas near the shore at night. Thus, people who swim or surf at night or during the dusk or early morning hours may encounter a tiger shark and are unlikely to see it before it attacks. The tiger shark's aggressive nature can also endanger people who happen to be in open ocean areas on boats. These sharks do not hesitate to closely follow boats or ships in hopes of eating garbage that is thrown overboard. One biologist reported that a tiger shark even tried to eat the propeller on his boat. Tiger sharks also do not hesitate to jump aboard fishing boats to grab people or animals to satisfy their hunger. According to *The Big Book of Sharks*, "The tiger shark's massive appetite increases the risk to humans."[6]

The tiger shark's aggressive behavior has led some people to kill them in retaliation for attacks on humans. In fact, after eight tiger shark attacks in Hawaii in the early 1990s, the Hawaii legislature introduced a bill to pay shark hunters to kill tiger sharks. The bill did not pass, in part because biologists argued that killing sharks would not solve the problem. Another factor that led to the bill's defeat was that Native Hawaiians traditionally revered tiger sharks, calling them "sacred aumakua, or guardian spirits,"[7] and opposed killing them. In addition, a local man named Jonathan Mozo, who survived an attack, encouraged the legislature to defeat the bill. Mozo later told *National Wildlife* magazine, "I have no feelings of hatred toward the shark. I don't want revenge. . . . We are not masters of the sea. If it were our territory, we'd have been born with gills and fins. I was out there a guest in his world."[8]

Chapter 3

Bull Shark

The bull shark was so named because its aggressive, unpredictable disposition is like that of a bull. It also head butts its prey like a bull does, and its stocky body reminds some people of a bull as well.

Biologists consider great white, tiger, and bull sharks to be the three species that are most likely to attack humans. Although there are more documented attacks on humans by great whites and tiger sharks, many experts believe the bull shark is the most dangerous shark to humans. This is because of its unpredictable, aggressive disposition and because it lives in freshwater rivers and lakes as well as in shallow ocean areas. People are thus likely to encounter bull sharks when swimming or surfing in oceans or freshwater bodies.

Shark experts also believe bull sharks are responsible for many attacks on humans that are blamed on other species. As the Florida Museum of Natural History explains, "The bull shark is not as easily identifiable as the white or tiger shark, so it is likely responsible for a large percentage of attacks with unidentified culprits."[9] Indeed, some biologists and historians believe a bull shark may have been responsible for the Jersey Shore shark attacks in 1916. These attacks are usually blamed on a great white that was later caught with human remains in its stomach. But a bull shark was also caught nearby, and some experts believe it may have done at least some of the damage.

Bull Shark Basics

The bull shark is generally 7 to 11 feet (2.1 to 3.4 m) long and weighs up to 700 pounds (317.5 kg). It has a stocky build; two short, wide dorsal fins; and a broad, flat snout. It has large, wide, triangular, serrated teeth on the upper jaw and narrow triangular teeth with small serrations on the bottom jaw. Its coloring is light gray to dark gray on top, with a lighter shade of gray on the belly.

At Home in Salt Water and Fresh Water

Bull sharks live in coastal areas in warm, shallow waters in the Pacific, Atlantic, and Indian Oceans. They are found from Baja California to Ecuador in the Pacific Ocean, anywhere from Massachusetts to Brazil in the western Atlantic Ocean, and from Morocco to Angola in the eastern Atlantic Ocean. They are also seen in the Indian Ocean from South Africa to Kenya as well as near India, and from Vietnam south to Australia. Bull sharks are rarely seen in water that is more than 500 feet (152 m) deep and prefer water temperatures that are around 80°F (26.7°C).

Bull sharks also live in freshwater rivers and lakes worldwide. In fact, they are one of the few species of sharks that can live in fresh water as well as salt water. Female bull sharks give birth to their young in estuaries or in freshwater rivers. The pups stay there for at least several years, since they cannot tolerate salt water until they mature. As they grow, they develop the ability to adapt to fresh water or salt water by changing the way their kidneys and other organs regulate the amount of water and salt in the body. Scientists believe this ability developed because it gives bull sharks a survival advantage. It allows babies to remain in shallow fresh water, away from larger sharks that might eat them, until they are big enough to fight off these large predators.

Bull sharks are often seen in the Brisbane River in Australia, the Amazon River in South America, Lake Nicaragua in Nicaragua, and the Ganges River in India. In the United States, they live in the Mississippi River, the Potomac River, and the Ohio River, and have been spotted as far north as Lake Michigan. After Hurricane Katrina in 2005, people saw many bull sharks in Lake Pontchartrain in Louisiana. Bull sharks had lived there for many years, but many people were unaware of them until the hurricane drove more of them into the lake from the Gulf of Mexico.

Hunting Habits

The bull shark is active during the day and night and usually hunts alone. Besides attacking animals to obtain food, it is also very territorial and will attack anything that enters what it considers to be its territory. Biologists find that bull sharks consider anywhere they happen to be as their territory, so they are basically always likely to attack.

The bull shark usually eats bony fish, other sharks, stingrays, sea turtles, sea birds, sea mammals, and dead animals. It is not afraid to attack creatures, including other sharks, that are bigger than it. In 1969 biologists learned of bull sharks' propensity to eat other larger sharks after Sea World in San Diego placed bull sharks

Sea life is abundant in the waters around Fiji, one of the places that is home to the bull shark (pictured). Bull sharks are uniquely suited to living in both salt water and fresh water.

in an enclosure with blue sharks, which range from 6 to 12 or more feet (1.8 to 3.7 m) long. The blue sharks did not last long.

Bull sharks that live in rivers and lakes feed on fish, crabs, turtles, and nonaquatic animals that are in or near the water (such as horses, dogs, cows, hippopotamus, deer, birds, and people).

The bull shark's senses of smell, hearing, lateral line, and electroreception all help it find prey. It often attacks in murky waters and does not depend on vision to hunt. It is also not a super-fast swimmer; its average swimming

THE BULL SHARK
AT A GLANCE

- Scientific name: *Carcharhinus leucas*
- Scientific family: Carcharhinidae
- Range: Worldwide
- Habitat: Warm, coastal ocean waters; warm freshwater estuaries, rivers, and lakes
- Size: Usually 7 to 11 feet (2.1 to 3.4 m)
- Weight: Up to 700 pounds (317.5 kg)
- Key features: Stocky build; broad, flat snout; dark gray color on top, lighter gray underneath
- Diet: Fish, other sharks, stingrays, turtles, sea birds, sea mammals, dead animals, nonaquatic animals in or near the water
- Deadly because: Teeth, aggression, territorial, found in warm, shallow ocean areas and freshwater lakes and rivers where people are
- Life span: About 12 years
- Conservation status: Near threatened

speed is 4.5 miles per hour (7.2 kph). However, it often chases its prey in bursts of speed. Once it reaches the prey, it often circles, then butts its head violently against the animal to stun it before attacking. Biologists call this the bump-and-bite technique. After bumping the prey, the shark bites into its flesh with the long, narrow, serrated teeth in the lower jaw. The lower teeth hold the prey while the shark shakes its head from side to side. The powerful, serrated upper teeth saw off chunks of flesh to swallow. Sometimes the shark will repeatedly take a bite, then circle again and take another bite.

Mostly Fearless and Aggressive

Part of what makes the bull shark a fearsome predator is that it is not picky about what it eats and is not afraid to attack creatures that can harm it. It thus has very few natural enemies that have a chance of winning a battle. These enemies include larger sharks such as the

Sharp, serrated teeth in the bull shark's upper and lower jaws (pictured) enable this powerful predator to hold on tight while it shakes its prey from side to side and then proceeds to saw off chunks of flesh.

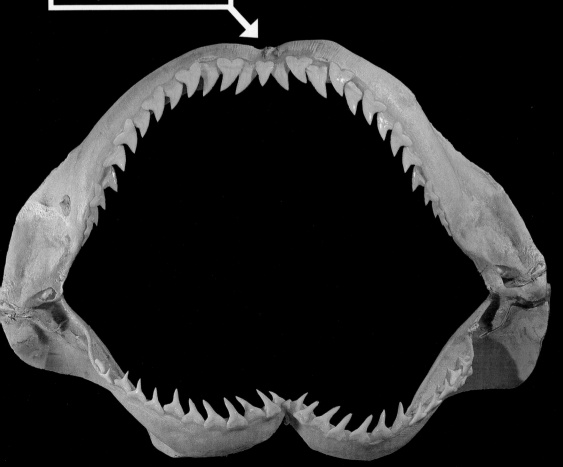

great white and tiger shark, larger bull sharks, and killer whales. In Australia, people have observed crocodiles eating bull sharks, so crocodiles seem to be another natural predator. Of all these predators, scientists have discovered that bull sharks seem to be most afraid of killer whales. Experiments show that when researchers play recorded sounds made by killer whales and other ocean creatures, bull sharks become extremely agitated by the killer whale sounds.

Despite this fear, biologist Steve Parker points out that "given their size and ferocity, few animals scare them."[10] In fact, the bull shark often manages to evade predators when it is attacked. It achieves this by regurgitating its stomach contents to distract the animal. The bull shark escapes while the predator eats whatever the bull shark has puked out. In some cases, an aggressive bull shark will simply attack a larger predator and not bother with trying to distract it. The fact that it functions well in murky water, when many other creatures cannot see well, greatly enhances these efforts. Even in clear water, the bull shark's darker color on top and lighter underside help camouflage it. When seen from above, the dark gray color helps it blend into the water below. When seen from below, the lighter belly blends into the sunlit water above. The bull shark's natural attributes thus work hand in hand with its aggressiveness to make it an apex predator.

Most Dangerous to Humans

These characteristics explain why many experts believe that the bull shark is the most dangerous shark to humans. Indeed, its aggressive nature and willingness to eat just about anything have led to many unprovoked at-

LIVING IN SALT WATER AND FRESH WATER

The bull shark's ability to adapt to fresh water and salt water comes from osmoregulation—the process by which the body regulates the amount of water and salt inside it. Osmoregulation depends on osmosis, which is the movement of water through tiny pores in a cell membrane. The water naturally moves from an area with small amounts of dissolved salt to an area with large amounts. This balances the concentration of salt inside and outside the cell. If these concentrations are not balanced, cells take in too much or too little water and die.

Sharks' kidneys are mostly responsible for osmoregulation. Most sharks can only osmoregulate in salt water, where their kidneys keep a high concentration of salt in the body so it can absorb enough water to live. If these sharks stayed in fresh water, their cells would absorb too much water and burst.

In contrast, bull sharks' kidneys gradually adapt to seawater or fresh water by changing the amount of salt and water the body retains. The kidneys remove more salt from the bloodstream in seawater than they do in fresh water. The shark also drinks more water and urinates approximately twenty times more in fresh water than in salt water to maintain the correct balance.

tacks on people who happen to be in or near the warm, shallow waters it prefers. In addition, doctors believe bull sharks are especially dangerous to people because the wounds they inflict are likely to become infected. This is because bull sharks often eat garbage and dead animals and live in polluted water. Doctors find that these wounds are also difficult to repair because the shark shakes its head rapidly while ripping out chunks of flesh.

In recent years, an increasing number of bull shark attacks have occurred in numerous areas. After six people died from six bull shark attacks at Second Beach in South Africa between 2007 and 2012, the beach ac-

A marine biologist observes the remains of a blacktip shark that was eaten by a giant bull shark. Bull sharks will attack most any prey, including other, larger sharks.

quired the reputation as the world's most dangerous beach. The sharks seem to be attracted to this beach because witch doctors in the area sacrifice animals and throw the carcasses into the water.

Another area that has seen many recent bull shark attacks is Reunion Island in the Indian Ocean. At least eighteen bull shark attacks and seven related deaths around this island between 2011 and 2013 led the government to ban swimming and surfing in these waters in 2013. Previously, Reunion Island was known as a surfer's paradise because of its perfect waves. But as of 2015, few surfers were coming to the island because of the ban, and several who defied it were attacked. In April 2015 thirteen-year-old Elio Canestru died after a bull shark attack, and in July 2015 another surfer lost his arm. Experts believe the increased number of bull sharks in the area have resulted from mud and debris washing into the ocean in recent years, making the water murky, which bull sharks like.

There have also been more bull shark attacks than usual in Florida, North Carolina, and South Carolina in the United States in 2014 and 2015. Biologists believe this may be because of unusually warm water, record numbers of swimmers, and more sea turtles than usual in the area. In June 2015 alone, ten people were attacked by bull sharks off the coasts of North and South Carolina. Fishermen have also reported seeing an unusually large number of bull sharks in these waters. Human activities, along with climate change, may be enhancing the dangers associated with this aggressive shark.

Chapter 4

Shortfin Mako

The shortfin mako is a fearsome predator that is dangerous to humans and to ocean life because it is the fastest shark and highly aggressive. It is always hungry, and often leaps out of the water into boats, where it is known to severely injure people.

Shortfin Mako Basics

The shortfin mako is usually 6 to 12 feet (1.8 to 3.7 m) long and weighs 330 to 1,100 pounds (150 to 499 kg). The largest known shortfin mako was 13 feet (4 m) long and weighed 1,250 pounds (567 kg).

This shark has a slender, streamlined body, a pointed wedge-shaped snout, large black eyes, five long gill slits, and a moon-shaped tail fin. Its color is metallic blue on the back and sides and white on the underside and mouth area. Its teeth are long, pointed, hook-like, and very sharp, but not serrated. It has about thirty teeth in each row of the upper and lower jaws. The teeth are visible even when the mouth is closed.

The "shortfin" part of the shortfin mako's name comes from the fact that its fins are shorter than those of many sharks, including its close relative the longfin mako. The shortfin mako's pectoral fins are less than 70 percent as long as its head. In comparison, the longfin mako's pectoral fins are longer than its head. In addition, one of the shortfin mako's two dorsal fins and the anal fin on the rear part of its underside are so short that it can be difficult to see them. The shark received the "mako" part of its name from the indigenous Maori people in New Zealand. *Mako* is the Maori term for shark.

At Home in the Sea

The shortfin mako is most likely to stay offshore in open oceans worldwide, though it is sometimes found closer to shore. It stays anywhere from the water's surface down to 2,500 feet (762 m) deep, depending on where food is located. It is usually most active at night.

This shark prefers temperatures between 63°F and 72°F (17°C to 22°C) and therefore inhabits warm to cool waters in the Pacific, Atlantic, and Indian Oceans and in the Mediterranean and Red Seas. It is most commonly seen in the southern portions of the Pacific and Atlantic Oceans, but has been spotted as far north as Great Britain in the eastern Atlantic Ocean, as far north as Canada in the western Atlantic Ocean, and as far north as Japan in the western Pacific Ocean. In 1998 scientists became aware that the shortfin mako sometimes migrates great distances in these oceans, presumably to find food or to mate. That year, Japanese researchers found a female shortfin mako in the northern Pacific Ocean. It had originally been tagged with a tracking device by biologists in California and had traveled more than 1,700 miles (2,736 km) that year. The fact that it is warm-blooded (like its close relative, the great white shark) and can keep its body temperature 12°F to 18°F (-11°C to -8°C) warmer than the surrounding water is

Despite its short fins, the slender, streamlined shortfin mako shark (pictured) is a fast swimmer. It also has an aggressive streak; shortfin makos have been known to jump out of the water and onto boats.

important in its ability to live in cool waters as well as warm ones.

Hunting Habits

The shortfin mako mainly preys on large fish such as tuna, bluefish, and swordfish; as well as on squid; sea turtles; marine mammals such as sea otters, seals, and porpoises; octopus; and smaller sharks. Like many shark species, mako pups often eat smaller siblings in the mother's womb before birth and after the pups are born.

Shortfin makos especially like to eat swordfish and bluefish. However, swordfish are likely to fight back with their swordlike bills when attacked. In fact, people have found many shortfin makos with a swordfish bill stuck in the gills or head. The shark survived after being impaled by the bill (and probably ate the rest of the swordfish).

Like other sharks, shortfin makos try to avoid encounters in which prey are able to fight back; prey that are sick or otherwise vulnerable make easier targets. For instance, they often attack swordfish when the fish are laying eggs. They are also likely to attack fish that are stuck in fishing nets.

The shortfin mako's brain, which is exceptionally large relative to its body size, is important in helping it locate and track down prey. The brain quickly coordinates input from the shark's keen senses of smell, hearing, and vision, and issues instructions to guide it in reaching and attacking its prey. Like many predatory sharks, the mako's sense of smell is especially acute. Studies show that it can smell one drop of blood in a million drops of water. It also relies on vision more than most sharks do. Its eyes have millions of light-sensitive cells called rods that allow it to clearly see shapes and movement in dim light. Unlike many sharks, however, shortfin makos do not rely on the detection of electrical signals to hunt.

The Attack

Once the shark senses its prey, its usual hunting strategy is to use its capacity for speed to chase and catch up with a potential meal. Its usual cruising speed is about 1.6 miles per hour (2.6 kph), but once it senses a prey animal, it quickly accelerates. As the fastest shark, it has been clocked swimming more than 45 miles per hour

THE SHORTFIN MAKO AT A GLANCE

- **Scientific name:** *Isurus oxyrinchus*
- **Scientific family:** Lamnidae
- **Range:** Worldwide
- **Habitat:** Tropical and temperate waters, near the shore; offshore; in open oceans
- **Size:** Usually 6 to 12 feet (1.8 to 3.7 m)
- **Weight:** Usually 330 to 1,100 pounds (150 to 499 kg)
- **Key features:** Pointed snout; moon-shaped tail; metallic blue on top and sides, white underneath; teeth are visible when the mouth is closed
- **Diet:** Fish such as tuna, bluefish, and swordfish; squid, sea turtles, marine mammals, octopus, smaller sharks
- **Deadly because:** Teeth, speed, aggression, huge appetite
- **Life span:** About 30 years
- **Conservation status:** Vulnerable

(72.4 kph). According to *The Encyclopedia of Sharks*, "It needs such speed because it feeds on other very swift swimmers, such as tuna, mackerel and swordfish."[11]

Once it can see its prey, it stalks it by swimming—with an open mouth—in a repeated figure-eight pattern. It usually swims under the animal, then shoots upward and opens its mouth wider. Since its upper and lower jaws move separately, when it opens its mouth, the shark tilts its head upward and pushes both jaws forward. This allows it to stab the prey with its long, pointed lower teeth while biting down with the upper teeth. Then it shakes its head wildly from side to side to help the upper teeth saw off chunks of flesh. Sometimes the mako swallows it whole. Since its flexible jaws let it open its mouth wide, the prey animal does not need to be especially small to be swallowed in one gulp. In one

The eye of the shortfin mako (pictured) contains millions of light-sensitive cells that enable the shark to see clear shapes and movement in dim light. The shark relies on this ability, along with other senses, to locate prey.

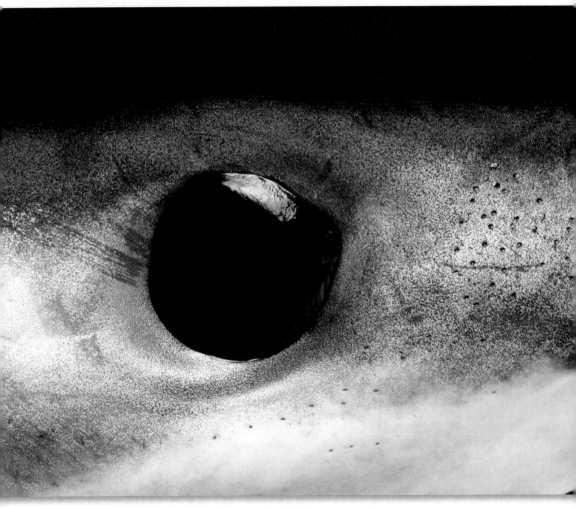

THE FASTEST SHARK

The shortfin mako's speed results from its warm-bloodedness and from factors that reduce drag. The shark's scientific name, *Isurus oxyrinchus*, helps explain what some of these drag-reducing factors are. *Isurus*, the Greek word for "equal tail," refers to the fact that the tail's top and bottom sections are the same size. The tail is also curved in a moon shape and is fairly flat. All these qualities allow the tail to push the shark ahead like an oar, counteracting drag from the water.

The second part of the name, *Oxyrinchus*, comes from the Greek words *oxy*, meaning sharp, and *rynchus*, meaning nose. The mako's sharply pointed nose, along with its streamlined body shape, also help reduce drag because water presses against narrow surfaces less than it does against wider surfaces.

Another critical factor that reduces drag and enhances speed is the mako's toothlike scales called dermal denticles. In 2012 and 2014 scientists led by George Lauder at Harvard University published studies that explained how the denticles in makos' skin achieve this feat. The researchers found that millions of these minute, sharp structures create tiny whirlpools of water that push the shark ahead as it swims.

documented case, a 740-pound (336 kg) shortfin mako swallowed a 120-pound (54 kg) swordfish in one piece. If the mako cannot swallow its prey whole, it bites off part of the animal such as the tail, which weakens the animal, then eats it in sections.

Dangers to Humans

The shortfin mako's speed, along with its huge, sharp teeth and aggressiveness, make it dangerous to people as well as to ocean animals. Since this shark usually stays in open ocean areas, most attacks on humans have been on deep-sea divers and people in boats. However, makos have also attacked people swimming near the shore. For example, a 6-foot (1.8 m) shortfin mako repeatedly attacked a young woman swimming in the northern Red Sea in 1974. It bit the woman twelve times on her arms and legs, and although she survived, doctors had to amputate one arm because it was so seriously damaged.

In addition to swimming fast, makos can leap more than 20 feet (6 m) out of the water when chasing prey and have attacked people after accidentally landing in boats during such a leap. Makos that are angry about being snared by a fishing hook are also known to jump into boats to attack people. In addition, when makos caught on a fishing line are reeled onto a boat they often continue to fight. This has resulted in many damaged boats and injured anglers. The ReefQuest Centre for Shark Research in Canada reports that shortfin makos can be so aggressive and frightening that "anglers who have suddenly found themselves sharing a boat with an aroused, thrashing mako have been known to leap into the water."[12] However, because many people enjoy eating mako meat, the sharks continue to be a prized catch in some regions.

Shortfin makos have also terrified people other than those who are fishing in boats. In 2012 the Australian photographer Sam Cahir had a run-in with a mako while on a boat photographing sharks in the Indian Ocean off the coast of Australia. The shark circled the boat for two hours and, Cahir told the *Daily Mail*, "made some menacing passes. On a number of occasions she almost swallowed the camera whole, allowing me to shoot straight down her maw [mouth]."[13] He also saw the mako push several great white sharks that were twice her size out of the way. She only left Cahir alone after he fed her a lot of fish, indicating that the fish on the boat were her target.

With prey in its sights, the shortfin mako opens its mouth wide, tilts its head upward, and pushes its jaws forward. The shark then stabs its prey with its long, pointed lower teeth and bites down with its upper teeth.

Indeed, the shortfin mako is literally hungry all the time. This is because its speed and the energy it needs to generate this speed make it necessary for it to eat about 3 percent of its body weight in food each day. The fact that the shark is warm-blooded also means it uses much energy to keep its body warm. Like other animals, the shortfin mako gets energy from the oxygen its blood carries to its cells and from the nutrients it obtains from food. Its vast energy needs fuel its insatiable appetite, which *The Big Book of Sharks* calls "bad news for the bony fish, porpoises, turtles, and birds it encounters."[14] Even though the mako does not seek to eat humans, its huge appetite, bad temper, and aggressiveness can also be bad news for people who get in its way.

Chapter 5

Common Thresher Shark

The common thresher shark usually stays in deep, open ocean areas. Because it does not live in areas where people swim and surf, it does not represent much of a threat to humans. This is not the case for its ocean-dwelling prey. Unlike most sharks, which are deadly primarily because of their teeth, the thresher shark is deadly at both ends because it also has a huge tail, which it uses as a weapon. The three species of thresher sharks are the only sharks that hunt with their tails. The common thresher, sometimes known as the fox shark or sea fox because of its long tail and crafty hunting methods, is the largest type of thresher shark.

Thresher Shark Basics

The common thresher's most prominent feature is the long upper lobe of its tail, which can be as long as its body. The lower tail lobe is a fraction of the length of the upper tail. The shark's full length, including the tail, can be up to 20 feet (6 m) and its weight up to 1,100 pounds (500 kg). Most common threshers are between 6.5 and 16 feet (2 to 4.9 m) long with an average weight of 767 pounds (348 kg).

The shark has one fairly tall and one short dorsal fin; a stout, torpedo-shaped body; small black eyes;

and a short, pointed snout. Its relatively small mouth contains teeth that are smaller than those of many sharks. However, the forty triangular teeth in the upper jaw and the forty-two in the lower jaw are curved with extremely sharp edges and can do major damage to prey.

The thresher's color is shiny brown, blue, gray, or black on top. Its sides are silver or copper, and the area of the sides above the pectoral fins is white. The underside ranges from pale gray or pale blue to white, with dark spots near the rear underside fins.

At Home in the Sea

The thresher shark lives in cool to warm waters worldwide. It migrates to warmer waters in autumn and back to cooler waters in spring before breeding during the summer. Threshers are found in the western Atlantic Ocean from Newfoundland down to Argentina and in the eastern Atlantic Ocean from Norway down to Ghana and the Ivory Coast. In the western Pacific Ocean, the thresher ranges from Australia to Japan and Korea. In the eastern Pacific Ocean, it is found from British Columbia to central Baja California and from Panama south to Chile. It also lives in the Mediterranean Sea and in the Indian Ocean from South Africa up to India. The thresher usually stays in open ocean areas on the surface down to about 1,800 feet (550 m), but sometimes ventures into shallow waters close to shore when hunting for food. Threshers also give birth in coastal areas and bays. Young threshers stay in these areas until they mature.

Hunting Habits

The thresher usually preys on schooling fish like blue-fish, herring, sardines, and mackerel. Sometimes it eats crustaceans, squid, octopus, and smaller sharks. It also eats sea birds on the water's surface. Like many sharks, developing threshers are known to eat other pups in the mother's uterus before birth.

The thresher usually hunts at night, using its senses of smell, its lateral line, and its ability to sense electric fields to find prey. It often swims long distances while hunting, and biologists have discovered that the muscles along its sides play an important role in allowing it to swim for long periods of time without becoming tired. These muscles are made of a type of muscle tissue known as red muscle. The red color comes from the rete mirabile—the mesh-like pattern of small blood vessels around the muscle that makes some sharks warm-blooded. However, truly warm-blooded sharks such as the great white and shortfin mako have retia mirabilia around the swimming muscles, internal organs, and eyes and brain. In contrast, the common thresher only has one set of these specialized blood vessels—the one around its swimming muscles. Scientists therefore do not consider it to be completely warm-blooded. Nonetheless, the thresher's rete mirabile is important because it carries a great deal of oxygen to the muscles and also retains the heat that warms these muscles. This allows the muscles to work continuously, even in cold water.

The Attack

Once the thresher finds its prey, its whiplike tail is central to its attack. Marine biologist Simon Oliver at the Univer-

The common thresher shark, seen here swimming in the Red Sea, has a long, narrow upper tail that it uses as a whip. The thresher usually hunts at night, often swimming long distances in search of prey.

sity of Liverpool and his colleagues, have studied thresher sharks for many years, and in 2013 they published the first-ever report describing details of its attack. The team found that the thresher typically swims quickly toward a school of fish, then stops suddenly, using its large pectoral fins as brakes. Then it lowers its snout and jerks the end of its tail. This causes the tail to swing over its head very rapidly and violently, hitting whatever fish are present. The tail's average speed is 30 miles per hour (48.3 kph), and the scientists clocked one shark whipping its tail at 80 miles per hour (128.8 kph). Large sharks whip their tails faster than smaller ones, since their tails are longer and generate more power.

The thresher tail usually whips several fish at a time, and the results are devastating. "We saw everything from swim bladder ruptures to broken spines to parts afloat,"[15] Oliver told *National Geographic*. Before Oliver's research,

A thresher shark embryo taken from the belly of another shark. Although threshers usually prey on schooling fish and other sea creatures, they also sometimes eat other thresher shark pups while still in the womb.

THE THRESHER SHARK
AT A GLANCE

- **Scientific name:** *Alopias vulpinus*
- **Scientific family: Alopiidae**
- **Range: Worldwide**
- **Habitat: Cool to warm waters; usually in open ocean areas**
- **Size: Usually 6.5 to 16 feet (2 to 4.9 m)**
- **Weight: Average 767 pounds (348 kg)**
- **Key features: Short, pointed snout; huge upper tail; shiny brown, blue, gray, or black color on top; paler colors to white underneath**
- **Diet: Mostly schooling fish like bluefish, herring, sardines, and mackerel; crustaceans, squid, octopus, sea birds, smaller sharks**
- **Deadly because: Whiplike long tail**
- **Life span: 40 to 50 years**
- **Conservation status: Vulnerable**

most experts believed thresher sharks usually killed or stunned prey by lashing the tail from side to side. But Oliver's team found that overhead lashes were far more common than sideways ones, especially on the first strike. Then the shark sometimes used a sideways tail lash to stun or kill more fish in the school. The researchers believe thresher sharks developed the ability to kill multiple prey animals this way because going after schooling fish one at a time is an inefficient method of hunting.

After hitting its prey, the shark swims around eating the dead or stunned fish. Sometimes teams of two or more threshers herd schools of fish into a small area, then whip away with their tails and share the prey. In other instances, groups of threshers cooperate and divide the tasks that are essential to corralling and killing the maximum number of fish. In this scenario, numerous sharks herd a school of fish into a small area. Then, several sharks continue circling around the school to keep it confined while other sharks kill fish with their tails. One or more sharks at a time then feed on the dead or weakened fish.

When scientists named the common thresher shark, they thought its method of attacking prey with the tail was sneaky, probably because most sharks attack with their teeth and do not herd prey cooperatively. Both words in the scientific name, *Alopias vulpinus*, mean "crafty fox." *Alopias* comes from the Greek word for fox, *alopex*. *Vulpinus* comes from the Latin word for fox, *vulpes*.

Threshers and Humans

Although they are deadly to sea life, thresher sharks are not usually aggressive toward humans. According to the Florida Museum of Natural History, "The species is shy and difficult to approach. Divers that have encountered these sharks claim that they did not act aggressively. However, some caution should be taken considering the size of these sharks. They have been known to attack boats."[16] These attacks on boats have usually been unprovoked. On the other hand, instances in which divers were attacked by a common thresher were all provoked by the divers threatening the shark with a spear gun or similar weapon. In addition, some divers have been injured by getting in the way when a thresher was whip-

A common thresher shark that was caught in a gill net is tossed ashore. Fishermen who accidentally catch threshers are sometimes injured as the shark lashes its long tail in a desperate effort to escape.

ping fish with its tail. Fishermen have also been injured by the tail when they caught a thresher in a net or with a hook and the shark lashed around trying to escape. The thresher is a popular fish among anglers because there is much demand for thresher meat, fins, liver oil (to use in vitamins), and skin (for use in leather products). The thresher shark's remarkable, powerful tail has also led to what biologists describe as questionable claims. In one widely circulated story, for instance, a group of anglers claimed that a 16-foot (5 m) common thresher

HOW THE THRESHER SHARK TAIL KILLS

Like thresher sharks, killer whales stun or kill fish with tail slaps. Scientists have proved that physical impact and cavitation underlie the effects of killer whales' tail strikes. Cavitation occurs when an object moves so fast that it changes the pressure in the water around it. The pressure change creates bubbles called cavitation bubbles. When the water pressure returns to normal, these bubbles explode, releasing tremendous amounts of noise and other energy. The energy creates a shock wave that can kill or seriously injure living creatures.

Cavitation has been studied most extensively in killer whales and in a 4-inch-long (10 cm) shrimp called the mantis shrimp. Mantis shrimp have oversized claws with a springlike part inside that snaps the claws so fast it creates cavitation bubbles. The resulting explosion kills the shrimp's prey, injures people who pick up mantis shrimp, and has even broken aquarium glass in places where these shrimp are kept in captivity.

Marine biologist Simon Oliver's research team at the University of Liverpool observed bubbles forming near the end of the fastest-moving thresher sharks' tails. Oliver believes this indicates that cavitation, along with physical impact, injures or kills threshers' prey, as happens with killer whales and mantis shrimp. However, no one has proved this theory, and further studies are under way.

decapitated a fellow angler with one stroke of its tail. They reported that the man leaned over the side of the boat to look at a fish he hooked, and the shark smacked him in the neck. His head apparently rolled over the side and vanished into the sea. Most shark experts, however, point out that this story has never been verified and express doubts that it actually happened. Shark expert R. Aidan Martin of the ReefQuest Centre for Shark Research, for example, wrote that "this story seems highly improbable."[17]

Another incident that some experts believe may not be accurate was described by biologist Russell J. Coles in 1914. Coles described how he observed a thresher shark off the coast of North Carolina using its huge tail to throw fish into its own mouth. Even though Coles was a biologist, numerous shark experts have stated that they doubt his story is true because no one else has reported similar thresher shark behavior. However, scientists acknowledge that there is still much to learn about this shark, so further observations may validate this claim.

Chapter 6

Spotted Wobbegong

The spotted wobbegong is in the family of carpet sharks that sit on the sea bottom and wait for prey to swim by, then ambush their meal. Experts do not consider this shark to be a major threat to humans, even though it does bite people if they step on it or happen to walk or swim near its home. The spotted wobbegong is also known to become aggressive if a diver or fisherman tries to spear it or catch it in a fishing net. Even though wobbegongs have never killed anyone, shark experts urge people to exercise caution around this shark. The International Shark Attack File has documented twenty-three spotted wobbegong attacks on humans, but biologists believe many other unreported attacks have occurred in areas where this shark lives.

Although the spotted wobbegong is not a major threat to humans, its remarkable camouflage tricks make it deadly to sea life. Instead of being an apex predator because of its speed, strength, and endurance, the wobbegong mostly achieves this status because of its ability to blend into its surroundings. It is thus known as an ambush predator.

Spotted Wobbegong Basics

The spotted wobbegong is the largest of the twelve species of wobbegong sharks. It is a medium-sized shark that usually ranges from 5 to 6.5 feet (1.5 to 2 m) long and weighs up to 175 pounds (79.4 kg). However, spotted wobbegongs have been officially documented as long as 10.5 feet (3.2 m) and weighing about 500 pounds (227 kg).

This shark has a flattened yellowish or greenish body and head with yellow, green, brown, white, and gray splotchy markings that match its surroundings. Its flat

With its flat body and splotchy yellow, brown, and green markings, the spotted wobbegong (pictured in Australian waters) bears little resemblance to other sharks. Its shape and coloring enhance its ability to ambush prey.

body and head and the splotchy color patterns that resemble a rug account for the spotted wobbegong's designation as a carpet shark.

The wobbegong's eyes are on top of its head. Its head also contains two rows of large fang-like teeth in the upper jaw and three rows in the lower jaw. Eight to ten fringe-like growths that look like seaweed fronds surround the shark's nose, mouth, and sides of the head. These prominent growths led to the name "wobbegong," which comes from an Australian Aboriginal term that means "shaggy beard." Part of the spotted wobbegong's scientific name, *Orectolobus maculatus*, also refers to these fringe-like growths. *Orectolobus* comes from the Greek words *orektos*, meaning "to stretch out," and *lobos*, meaning lobes or growths. The other part of the scientific name, *maculatus*, comes from the Latin word *maculosus*, which means spotted.

The spotted wobbegong's fins are comparatively much smaller than those of sharks that are built for speed and endurance. Since this shark spends most of its time sitting on the seafloor, its two short dorsal fins, short tail fin, and longer, broad pectoral fins are designed to help it move around on the sand, rocks, and reefs where it stays. In particular, the wobbegong's pectoral fins are located on its sides to help it scoot along the sea bottom. In contrast, the pectoral fins of fast-swimming sharks are located on the underside. The wobbegong's pectoral fins also give it a boost when it shoots rapidly upward or sideways to snare a meal.

At Home in the Sea

The spotted wobbegong lives in warm to temperate shallow waters in the eastern Indian Ocean around Australia. It also lives near Japan and in the South China

THE SPOTTED WOBBEGONG AT A GLANCE

- **Scientific name:** *Orectolobus maculatus*
- **Scientific family:** Orectolobidae
- **Range:** Eastern Indian Ocean around Australia; near Japan; in the South China Sea
- **Habitat:** Shallow water, rocky and coral reefs, sandy areas, lagoons, under piers, in estuaries, and in tide pools
- **Size:** Usually 5 to 6.5 feet (1.5 to 2 m)
- **Weight:** Usually up to 175 pounds (79.4 kg)
- **Key features:** Flattened body and head; fringe-like growths on the head; yellowish or greenish color with multicolored splotches
- **Diet:** Bony fish like sea bass; crustaceans like crab and lobster; octopus; eels; rays; other sharks
- **Deadly because:** Camouflage, teeth, mouth suction, fast strike
- **Life span:** As long as 30 years
- **Conservation status:** Near threatened

Sea. It is found in rocky and coral reefs, sandy areas, sea grass beds, lagoons, estuaries, under piers, and in tidepools. Sometimes it is found in extremely shallow water that barely covers its body.

This shark is usually active at night and rests in undersea caves, in shipwrecks, or under rocky overhangs in rocky and coral reefs during the day. Scientists and divers have observed that individual spotted wobbegongs tend to stay in one area and claim a particular cave or other resting place as their own for long periods of time—even for several years. Divers in particular have noted that they find certain individual wobbegongs resting in the same cave or reef during consecutive diving expeditions. Biologists call this behavior site attachment. The book *Ecology of Australian Temperate Reefs* explains that wobbegongs probably choose a sheltered resting place and return to it for safety reasons, "to avoid larger shark predators, such as tiger sharks, bull sharks and white sharks."[18]

Hunting Habits

The spotted wobbegong mostly eats rays, eels, octopus, crustaceans like crab and lobster, and bony fish like sea bass. It also eats smaller sharks, including pups of its own species. In fact, biologists have noticed that wobbegong pups swim away from their mother immediately after birth because she is likely to eat them if they stay around.

The wobbegong usually hunts at night. Sometimes it slowly sneaks up on its prey before attacking, but usually it sits motionless on the sea bottom, well camouflaged in the sand, rocks, plants, and shells around it. Although it is not moving around, the wobbegong's senses of sight, smell, hearing, lateral line, and electroreception remain alert for prey above and around itself. Having eyes on top of its head gives the shark a good view of everything above and around it, so sight plays a big role in its quest for food.

The wobbegong's ampullae of Lorenzini are also located on the top of its head and snout to help it sense prey that pass by overhead. Since it does not actively hunt, this shark only relies on electroreception to detect creatures that are a few feet away. It thus has fewer am-

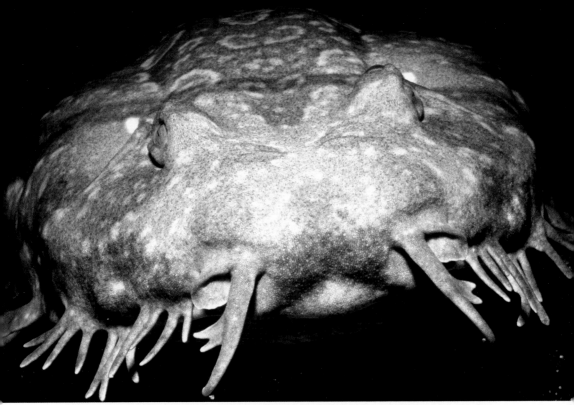

The eyes of the spotted wobbegong, located on top of its head, provide the shark with a good view of possible prey. Before it strikes, the wobbegong creates a distraction by wiggling the seaweed-like fringe on its head.

pullae than sharks that actively hunt. While sharks like the great white have approximately fifteen hundred ampullae, the spotted wobbegong only has a few hundred of these cells. Unlike most sharks, the wobbegong also has a special cluster of ampullae called a hyoid cluster. This is located behind the first gill slit on both sides of the head. Researchers at the University of Western Australia believe the location of the hyoid cluster suggests that it may help the wobbegong detect predators, rather than prey, that are approaching from the sides. However, no one has proved this theory.

Once the wobbegong senses a prey animal nearby, it often wiggles the seaweed-like fringe on its head to distract the animal. Then, when the prey is about 2 feet (60 cm) away from its head, the shark suddenly shoots upward or sideways "with mind-stuttering swiftness"[19] to grab the animal with its fang-like teeth, according to the ReefQuest Centre for Shark Research. This strike only takes about twenty-five milliseconds.

Multitasking Teeth and Vacuum-Like Suction

The fang-like teeth are very important in the spotted wobbegong's ability to prey on the creatures it likes to eat. These teeth are razor sharp and curved, which allows the shark to easily grab and gobble up slippery fish. The teeth are also designed to crush and grind up the shells of crustaceans like crab and lobster. At the same time as the teeth grab the prey, the wobbegong's mouth, throat, and gill muscles expand to help it trap and quickly ingest its meal. The expanding muscles create a suction-like force that pulls the prey into the mouth and leaves no chance of escape. The shark then swallows the prey whole.

Scientists have also observed the spotted wobbegong using its mouth vacuum to suck prey out of crevices in rocks or coral. When its ampullae of Lorenzini sense prey hiding in these crevices, the shark presses its head against the rock or coral opening and opens its mouth to activate the suction force. This pulls the prey into its mouth.

Although spotted wobbegongs rarely bite humans, when they do so their teeth and vacuum-like mouth suction can do major damage. Indeed, people's limbs have had to be amputated after being chewed up by

SPOTTED WOBBEGONG BREATHING TOOLS

Many sharks, such as the great white and mako, must keep swimming to breathe. This is because their gills do not work unless forward motion forces water into the mouth and through the gills. The gills separate oxygen from the water and send the oxygen to blood vessels to distribute to body parts. Unneeded water exits through the gill slits.

Unlike these sharks, spotted wobbegongs and other bottom-dwelling sharks have two breathing tools that let them sit motionless on the sea bottom and wait for prey. The first tool is a crescent-shaped hole called a spiracle behind each eye. Water flows into the spiracles, which are connected to tubes that send the water through the gills for oxygen extraction. The shark can thus breathe, even when its mouth is closed.

The second tool is the buccal muscles in the shark's cheeks. These muscles pull water into the mouth and over the gills even when the shark is motionless. Spotted wobbegongs can use the spiracles and/or the buccal muscles to breathe. Some sharks, such as the sand tiger and lemon shark, can breathe like great whites while swimming; and like wobbegongs, using their buccal muscles, while resting.

this shark's sharp teeth. Wobbegongs also do not like to let go once they have latched onto a human, and scientists believe the shark's mouth suction contributes to this behavior. In one instance in 2004, a spotted wobbegong attacked a man named Luke Tresoglavic in Australia while he was snorkeling. It bit him on the leg and would not let go, so he swam to shore with the shark attached to his leg. Three lifeguards managed to pry the shark off, but it was not easy. One lifeguard grabbed the shark's upper jaw. Another grabbed the lower jaw, and the third poured water into the gills. The shark finally released Tresoglavic's leg, leaving him with about seventy

A spotted wobbegong opens its mouth wide and expands its throat to trap a meal. The opening of the mouth creates a suction-like force that draws in prey, which can then be swallowed whole.

puncture wounds. Fortunately, he did not need surgery.

Other people attacked by spotted wobbegongs have experienced even worse injuries. In 2014, for example, a spotted wobbegong grabbed the foot of a thirteen-year-old surfer named Kirra-belle Olsson at a beach in Australia. Its teeth left huge gashes that required surgery to repair the damage. Olsson told newspaper reporters that not only did the shark bite her foot three times, but it also "tried to pull me under."[20] She managed to free herself from the shark and paddled to shore, screaming. Family members rushed her to a hospital, where a shark expert confirmed that the bites came from a spotted wobbegong. In other attacks on humans, people have reported that the spotted wobbegong's flexible body allowed it to swing its head upward to bite the hand of an individual who was holding the shark by the tail. Although the wobbegong is not deadly to humans, it still possesses the qualities that make it an apex predator in its habitat.

Source Notes

Introduction: Apex Predators

1. National Oceanic and Atmospheric Administration, "NOAA Fisheries Fact Sheet—Bull Shark." www .nmfs.noaa.gov.
2. Leonard Compagno, Marc Dando, and Sarah Fowler, *Sharks of the World*. Princeton, NJ: Princeton University Press, 2005, p. 53.

Chapter 1: Great White Shark

3. Steve Parker, *The Encyclopedia of Sharks*. Buffalo, NY: Firefly, 2008, p. 83.
4. Discovery Communications, *The Big Book of Sharks*. New York: Time Home Entertainment, 2012, p. 29.

Chapter 2: Tiger Shark

5. Parker, *The Encyclopedia of Sharks*, p. 147.
6. Discovery Communications, *The Big Book of Sharks*, p. 26.
7. Michael Tennesen, "A Killer Gets Some Respect," *National Wildlife*, August 1, 2000. www.nwf.org.
8. Quoted in Tennesen, "A Killer Gets Some Respect."

Chapter 3: Bull Shark

9. Florida Museum of Natural History, "Bull Shark." www .flmnh.ufl.edu.
10. Parker, *The Encyclopedia of Sharks*, p. 58.

Chapter 4: Shortfin Mako

11. Parker, *The Encyclopedia of Sharks*, p. 146.
12. R. Aidan Martin, "Biology of the Shortfin Mako (*Isurus oxyrinchus*)," ReefQuest Centre for Shark Research. www.elasmo-research.org.
13. *Daily Mail Online*, "That's One Bad Fish: Photographer Gets Shot of a Lifetime After Short-Tempered Shark Circles His Boat for Two Hours," October 24, 2012. www.dailymail.co.uk.
14. Discovery Communications, *The Big Book of Sharks*, p. 21.

Chapter 5: Common Thresher Shark

15. Quoted in Ed Yong, "Thresher Sharks Hunt with Huge Weaponised Tails," *National Geographic*, July 10, 2013. http://phenomena.nationalgeographic.com.
16. Florida Museum of Natural History, "Thresher Shark." www.flmnh.ufl.edu.
17. R. Aidan Martin, "Biology of the Common Thresher (*Alopias vulpinus*)," ReefQuest Centre for Shark Research. www.elasmo-research.org.

Chapter 6: Spotted Wobbegong

18. Scoresby Shepherd and Graham Edgar, eds., *Ecology of Australian Temperate Reefs*. Collingwood, Victoria: Csiro, 2013, p. 409.
19. R. Aidan Martin, "Spotted Wobbegong," ReefQuest Centre for Shark Research. www.elasmo-research.org.
20. Quoted in Melanie Kembrey, "Teen Girl 'Bitten by Shark' While Surfing at Avoca Beach," *Newcastle Herald* (Newcastle, Australia), October 17, 2014. www.theherald.com.au.

camouflage: Something that blends into the environment.

cavitation: The formation of explosive bubbles in water due to changes in water pressure.

crustacean: A sea creature like lobster, crab, and shrimp that has a hard shell.

dermal denticles: Toothlike scales in shark skin.

drag: A force, such as that exerted by water, that presses against a moving object and slows it down.

electroreception: The ability to sense small electric fields.

estuary: A partly enclosed body of water with a low salt content, in between an ocean and a freshwater river or lake.

osmosis: The natural movement of water through a cell membrane to an area with a higher concentration of dissolved substances.

rete mirabile: A mesh-like structure made of small blood vessels that surrounds some sharks' organs and makes the shark warm-blooded.

satellite tracking device: A device scientists attach to an animal to study its behavior via signals the device sends to satellites that orbit Earth, which in turn send signals to a specific computer.

school: A group of fish of one species.

serrated: Jagged, with sawlike edges.

spiracle: A crescent-shaped hole and tube behind the eyes of bottom-dwelling sharks that help them breathe while holding still.

temperate: Areas that are cool to fairly warm.

territorial: Protective of one's living area.

For Further Research

Books

Discovery Channel, *Sharkopedia*. Des Moines, IA: Discovery Communications, 2013.

Derek Harvey, *Super Shark Encyclopedia*. New York: DK, 2015.

Tom Jackson, *Ferocious Sharks*. New York: Stevens, 2011.

Ruth Musgrave, *Everything Sharks*. Washington, DC: National Geographic Kids, 2011.

Internet Sources

CBS News, "Five Most Dangerous Sharks to Humans," 2015. www.cbsnews.com/pictures/five-most-dangerous-sharks-to-humans.

Diana Gerstacker, "The Most Dangerous Beaches for Shark Attacks in the U.S.," *Huffington Post*, July 5, 2015. www.huffingtonpost.com/the-active-times/the-most-dangerous-beaches-for-shark-attacks_b_7708416.html.

Jennifer Viegas, "Three Deadliest Sharks Named," *Discovery News*, August 11, 2014. http://news.discovery.com/animals/sharks/three-deadliest-sharks-named-140811.htm.

Websites

Global Shark Attack File (www.sharkattackfile.net). This website tracks worldwide shark attacks on humans, specifying the type of shark involved, where the attack occurred, the type of injury, and whether the attack was provoked or unprovoked.

International Shark Attack File, Florida Museum of Natural History (www.flmnh.ufl.edu). The International Shark Attack File investigates shark bite incidents and determines the cause. It also tracks statistics on shark attacks and provides information on avoiding such attacks, along with detailed information about sharks.

ReefQuest Centre for Shark Research (www.elasmo-research.org). The ReefQuest Shark Research Centre website provides detailed information on all aspects of shark biology and behavior.

The Shark Foundation (www.sharkfoundation.org). The Shark Foundation is dedicated to protecting and conducting research on sharks. Its website offers information on many types of sharks and the threats they pose and face.

Sharks World (www.sharks-world.com). The Sharks World website contains detailed information about many species of sharks, including their biology, behavior, habitats, evolution, and conservation efforts.

Index

Picture Credits

Melissa Abramovitz is an award-winning author who specializes in writing nonfiction books and magazine articles for all age groups, from preschoolers through adults. She also writes some fiction, poetry, and picture books and is the author of a book and numerous other educational materials for writers.